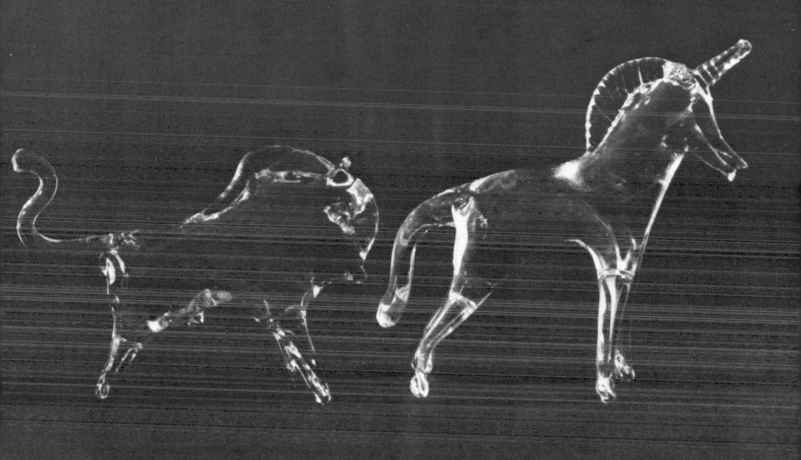

THE SEE-THROUGH ZOO

THE SEE-THROUGH ZOO

■ HOW GLASS ANIMALS ARE MADE ■

written and photographed by

Suzanne Haldane

PANTHEON BOOKS

New York

FOR TOM

My sincere thanks to these people at The Pilgrim Glass Corporation:
Alfred E. Knobler, Eugene Miller, Arnold Russell,
Mario Sandon, and Jerry Combs. Also Jeanne Dale, Danny Francis,
Robbie Lakes, Oscar Napier, David Parsons,
Brenda Thompson, and Felicia Toretto. And thanks to all who helped,
especially Agnes H. Cooper, Todd Cooper, Jason Cox,
Kassandra Duane, Cathy Moore, Jane Wilson, and Tom Hyman.

The photographs on page 8 and 9 (left) are courtesy
New York Public Library.

Library of Congress Cataloging in Publication Data
Haldane, Suzanne.   The see-through zoo.
Summary: Text and photographs introduce the art
of making glass animals, a very delicate craft requiring careful timing.
1. Glass blowing and working — Juvenile literature.
2. Animals in art — Juvenile literature.
[1. Glass craft.   2. Animals in art]   I. Title.
TP859.H24   1984   748.8   83-13122
ISBN 0-394-85497-7
ISBN 0-394-95497-1 (lib. bdg.)

THE SEE-THROUGH ZOO

BEHIND THE DOORS of a hot, noisy glass factory something exciting is going on. While familiar vases and baking dishes are being made, skilled craftsmen are also creating glass animals.

These glass creatures are made differently from vases and dishes. To make a vase, a glassblower winds hot glass onto the end of a blowpipe. With puffs of his breath, he inflates the glass until it becomes a large bubble, which he then shapes into a vase. Baking dishes are made simply by pouring hot glass into a mold. Glass animals, however, are made by hand, from solid balls of molten glass which a glassmaker pulls and pushes into shape with special tools.

To have a quiet look at these animals, it's best to visit the factory's showroom, where beasts of all kinds are exhibited under glowing spotlights.

 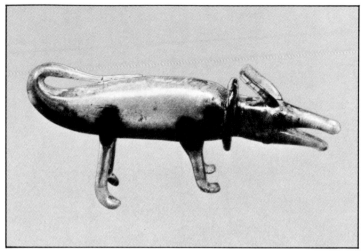

Glass is made from materials that could be found in any backyard: sand, soda ash, and lime. Yet from these familiar ingredients, objects both ordinary and unique have been fashioned for many thousands of years.

The Egyptian glass pig on the left is over two thousand years old. And his companion on the right was made fifteen hundred years ago, in the Roman Empire.

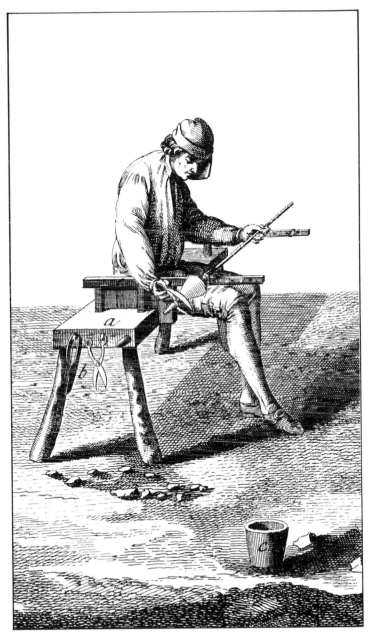

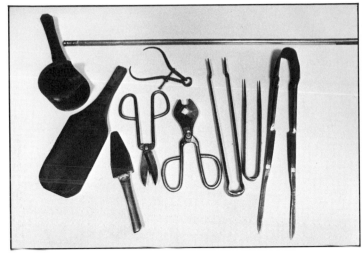

In this French drawing, from an eighteenth-century encyclopedia, a glassmaker sits at his workbench. Glass is made today much the way it was centuries ago.

Today's glassmakers use the same simple tools.

The main ingredient in the ancient recipe is still sand, like that found on the beach. Glassmakers call it silica, and they use a specially pure kind, found in Africa and various parts of the United States. It is brought by truck to the glass factory and vacuum-fed through long pipes to a silo on the roof.

Inside the factory, a mixing machine resembling a giant cement mixer stands ready to receive the ingredients. Silica, soda ash, and lime travel from the silo down a long tube into the mixer.

Dials to the left of the mixer control the amount of sand, soda ash, and lime that is added. Inside the mixing machine, eight sets of cutting blades stir the ingredients together. The dry mixture is called the batch.

Silica, lime, and soda ash alone produce a greenish glass; so at this point, small amounts of other chemicals are added to the batch by hand. These additional chemicals prevent the green color from forming, and the result is a clear, brilliant glass known as crystal.

The batch is loaded into a special cart and wheeled down a long, dark corridor toward the furnace where it will be melted. As the cart approaches the furnace, the air becomes noticeably hotter, and a deafening, nonstop roar blots out all other sound. The noise is made by the gas burners that heat the furnace.

In a large open area, several paces from where the craftsmen work, the furnace is fired up to the melting temperature of 2,600° F—more than ten times the heat needed to boil water.

At night, while the glassmakers are home sleeping, the batch is cooked. During the ten to twelve hours it takes to fuse—melt and blend—the ingredients, the intense heat must be kept constant, or the furnace will be damaged and the glass ruined.

The fire never goes out, but when the batch is done, and the impurities have been skimmed off the top, the temperature is lowered slightly to 2,000° F.

Too hot ever to touch, the molten glass, now referred to as "metal," is ready to be worked.

Two people are needed to turn metal into animals. One is the teacher, the other the pupil.

The master craftsman is called the gaffer, from an old English word meaning grandfather. He has had years of experience and familiarity with glass. Guided only by his imagination, he pulls and pushes the glass into the shapes of more than fifty different animals, using a variety of tools.

His helper, called a gatherer because he collects or gathers the glass, assists and learns from the master.

The gatherer starts the process. He selects an iron rod called a punty rod, nearly as long as he is tall. Standing behind the corrugated steel sheets at the sides of the oven, which help shield him from the intense temperatures, he thrusts the rod into the fiery inferno. By twirling the rod around as he twists it upward, he gathers a taffylike ball of molten glass. From this point on, his punty rod must be kept spinning, or the pull of gravity will cause the hot glass to sag and drip.

While the gatherer does all of his work standing up, the gaffer needs to sit at a bench to do his. The specially designed gaffer's bench is similar to those used by glassmakers long ago. Its two wooden arms are topped with steel, and a crescent-shaped shield extends down from one arm to protect the gaffer's legs.

The tools he will need are spread out beside him, within easy reach. Buckets of water stand nearby. From time to time, he will dip his tools into the water to cool them off.

The two artisans must work fast. They are always racing against time, because glass cools rapidly, and below a certain temperature it can no longer be shaped.

Tiny animals may be pulled and pinched into shape in a matter of seconds. But larger animals, especially those composed of several pieces of metal, must be reheated before the addition of each piece, because hot glass will only stick to hot glass.

When a piece is finished, it is carried to a special oven called a lehr, where it rides on a conveyor belt through chambers of decreasing temperatures, so that it may cool down gradually. When glass is cooled too quickly, the outside cools faster than the inside, and the piece breaks.

Color guides the glassmakers through their work. When glass is taken from the furnace, it is cherry red. While being worked it turns amber. As it becomes paler in color, it becomes harder to work. Only after it has cooled does it become clear and colorless.

The gaffer's years of practice have taught him to concentrate completely on what he is doing and to work without wasting a second. In a few moments he turns a shapeless blob of glass into a recognizable figure.

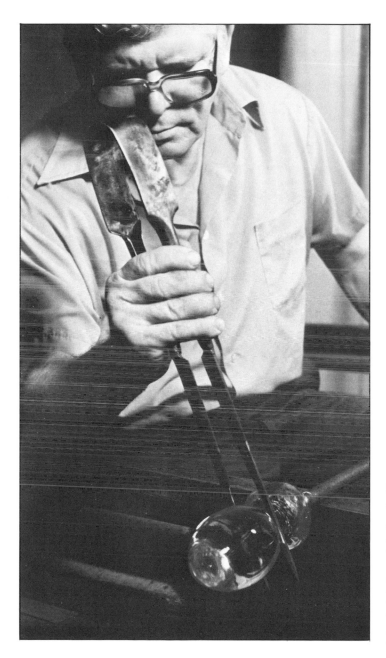

An animal starts as a ball of molten glass. The gaffer begins most animals at either the head or tail. Cats, horses, and unicorns begin at the head; dolphins, sharks, and seals at the tail.

When making an elephant, however, the gaffer begins with the body. He rotates the hot glass and shapes it with a steel tool that looks like a giant pair of tweezers.

 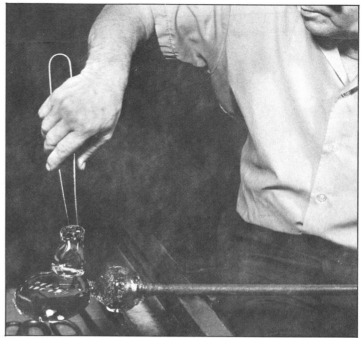

Most animals are made from one piece of glass, but it takes eleven separate pieces to make an elephant. While the gaffer keeps the body in motion, the gatherer brings him a gob of glass for a leg. Once the leg is joined to the body, the gaffer snips off the excess with a pair of shears. Then he shapes the elephant's foot.

These steps are repeated until all four legs are in place.

At this point, the gaffer reheats the piece, because it has cooled too much to allow more metal to stick.

When the gaffer gets back to his bench with the warmed sculpture, the gatherer brings a ball of glass for the head. The gaffer steadies and guides the rod with a special pair of shears called bit shears and allows the masses to join.

As the gatherer pulls the glass away from the head, the trunk is fashioned. The gaffer watches and readies his shears to snip off the glass when it has reached the proper length.

Next, the gaffer creates a mouth by indenting the glass with his shears.

The gatherer adds one tusk, then the other, as the gaffer steadies the piece. While the gatherer returns to the furnace for more glass, the gaffer shapes each tusk before it becomes too cool.

When work is done by hand, there are some days when it goes better than others. On a bad day the gaffer may have to discard several pieces. The rejected figures become part of an assortment of broken fragments called cullet. The cullet can be saved, remelted, and used again.

And sometimes, if the gaffer's concentration is interrupted and the animal cools too quickly, the glass just cracks and shatters into an unrecognizable form. Such unfortunate, misshapen creatures never leave the factory. They, too, become cullet.

But there are times when glass has to be thrown away. If impurities creep into the batch because of fluctuating melting temperatures or dust in the air, they can cause flaws that ruin the magical qualities of the glass.

Here, air bubbles, called "seeds," have caused these birds to be eliminated from the glassmaker's menagerie. Only the best animals carry the factory's label.

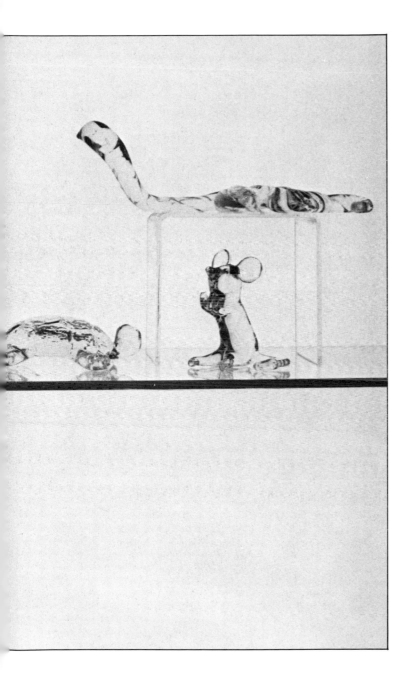

Animals of every sort belong to the see-through zoo. Here otter (*above*), pig, deer, cat, snail, turtle, snake (*above*), and mouse make up this display.

Solid glass, yet fragile enough to be broken into a thousand pieces, animals such as these have been collected for hundreds of years. People of all ages have been fascinated by their forms and their ability to both capture and reflect light, but few have been able to watch how the animals were made.

Watching craftsmen shape common materials into something of beauty is always enjoyable, especially when speed and precision are part of the art. The glass animal maker possesses a rare skill, and with it he produces creatures that are all individual sculptures —each one a unique member of the see-through zoo.

AFTERWORD

All the photographs in this book were taken at the Pilgrim Glass factory in Cerado, West Virginia. Mario Sandon, the gaffer, came to West Virginia in 1962 from Murano, Italy, a small island well known for its production of fine glassware. Now, forty years after he first worked glass, he is solely responsible for the menagerie that caries the Pilgrim label. His helper says, "Mario can make any kind of animal, vase, or bowl, in any design. He's a real artist!"

Mr. Sandon's gatherer is Jerry Combs. He was born in Kentucky and has been an assistant for several years. He vows he will become a gaffer someday.

About Jerry Combs, Mario Sandon says, "Not everyone is suitable to be a gaffer's assistant. You have to have a patient manner that allows you to spend years at practice, an enthusiasm for the work—and a special talent. Jerry has all these."

Pilgrim welcomes visitors to watch these two glassmakers work. Their animals are sold, inexpensively, in stores throughout the country.

SUZANNE HALDANE grew up in Princeton, New Jersey. Her photographs have been exhibited at the Catskill Center for Photography and have appeared in books and in national and regional magazines. Ms. Haldane divides her time between New York City and the mountains near Woodstock, New York.

Gr 4+

Craft
glassblowing

1984

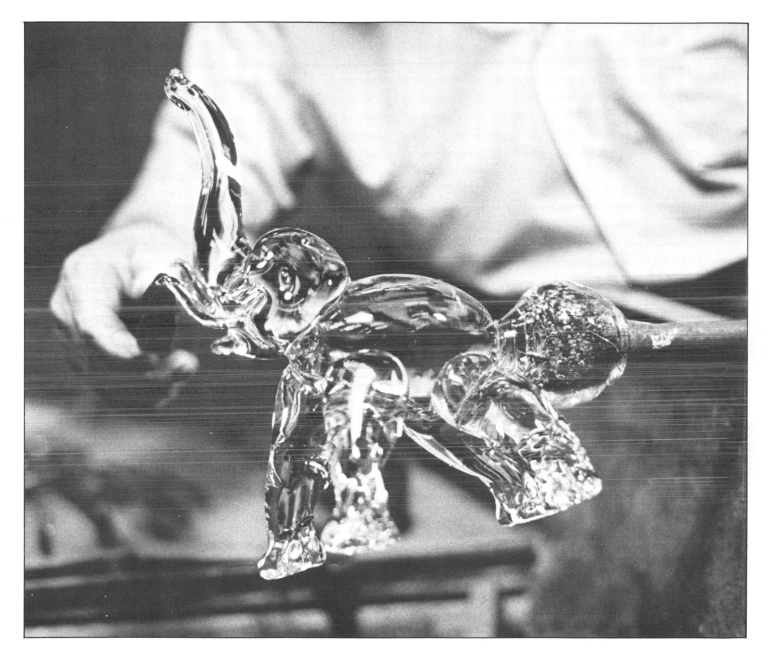

As they do their jobs, the gaffer and his gatherer perform a kind of dance. The steps and rhythm are defined by the particular animal they are forming.

The gatherer's most important responsibility is to anticipate his gaffer's moves. An incorrect decision could put him in the wrong place at the wrong moment, and the glass could be ruined because too much time is lost. When he notices the master making the final gestures that complete a piece, he must hand the gaffer a new ball of hot glass. Quickly, he must remove the finished beast and get back to the furnace to gather more glass for the next animal.

Each man must be alert and always aware that he has scorching hot glass on the end of his rod. If the molten glass ever touched skin, it would cause serious burns.